PATCHCRAFTS

This edition published 1977 by
Wayland (Publishers) Limited
49 Lansdowne Place, Hove, East Sussex BN3 1HF

SBN 85340 499 2

Filmset by Filmtype Services Limited, Scarborough
Printed in Italy by New Interlitho SpA

Beginning Crafts Series
Created and produced by Sackett Publishing Services Ltd
2 Great Marlborough Street London W1

Photography by Robert Glover Studios, Amersham, Bucks
Series Editor: Eve Harlow

Beginning Crafts

PATCHCRAFTS

Eve Harlow

Illustrated by Marion Mills

Wayland Publishers England

Contents

Introduction to patchwork

Putting patches on clothing is a technique almost as old as civilization. Primitive women must have tried to repair holes with scraps of hide and fur and eventually, from the need to mend garments to make them last longer came the desire to make the patches look more attractive. The art of patchwork appliqué was a natural evolution and the craft appears to have been known and practised for thousands of years. The earliest known example is a funeral canopy made of tiny pieces of gazelle skin, stitched together and embroidered. It was found in Egypt and has been dated at around 980 BC – almost 3000 years ago.

Appliqué is supposed to have been introduced into Europe by the Crusaders who saw examples of the technique in the middle east. During the middle ages, appliqué and pieced patchwork was used extensively for heraldic embroidery, and for making banners, surcoats, ceremonial robes and military apparel of all kinds.

Born of thrift

With the invention of weaving, patchwork began to have an impact on domestic needlewomen. New types of materials began to be imported from the East – lightweight cottons, linens and muslins. Later, when engraved copper plates began to be used for printing, patterned fabrics became more common and two or three colours were used in designs. Unlike embroidery, patchwork appealed to both ladies and their maidservants. For both it was a pleasant and thrifty occupation. Fragments of material left over from the household's sewing were stitched into decorative patterns and from the big houses, the craft spread into the village homes. Although most of the patchwork produced in Britain at this time was used for making quilts, other furnishings were also made – bed curtains for instance and stool covers – and well-preserved examples can be seen in museums.

However, it was in America that patchwork developed into a folk art, with a style which is distinctive and a technique that is different from that of the traditional patchwork of Europe.

American patchwork

Piecing quilts is regarded as an American needlecraft and over 300 years it has developed into an art form. The pioneer women who sailed from the Old World to America took their skills and knowledge of sewing with them but once there, the pattern of their lives changed drastically and so did their approach to sewing. The settlers were poor and everything that they carried with them to America had to last because there was no way of replacing clothes when they wore out. The ships from England carried tools, seeds, building materials and ploughshares and there was no room for anything which was not essential. So clothes were mended and patched and then, when they wore beyond repair, the good parts were cut away and then stitched together again to make new fabric. The winters in the new country were long and cold and warm quilts were needed for the beds. So making quilts, patching the scraps together, became the occupation for winter evenings, sitting by the log fire. The lives of these hardworking women had little in them that was lighthearted or beautiful and so their creativity found expression in the stitching of their quilts. The patterns they invented record their impressions of the new land, the hopes and fears, their religious beliefs and their sense of beauty. The patterns are charming and are still being copied today.

Materials, tools and equipment

Fabrics for patchwork
Ideally, the fabrics for patchwork should be pieces from the ragbag, scraps from dressmaking sessions, cuttings from discarded clothes and remnants from sales. This is the traditional way of obtaining fabrics for patchwork because the craft has its origins in thriftiness. However, modern patchwork is often worked in new fabrics and certainly, it is very much more satisfying to be able to choose just the colours and patterns you want for a patchwork project.
Generally speaking, fabrics for patchwork should be firm in weave and should not fray. Cotton is the most popular fabric for these reasons. Most fabrics can be used for patchwork as long as they are not too thick or too fine but there are certain rules to be observed in choosing and using them.
1 Never mix fabrics of different weights and thickness. Never use cotton and silk together in one piece of patchwork. The cotton is the stronger weave and will pull away from the silk, spoiling your work.
2 Test for colourfastness if you are in any doubt about a fabric. Fabrics should be pre-shrunk if the item is going to be laundered but if a mixture of fabrics is being used, such as in a crazy quilt, the quilt should be dry-cleaned.
3 You can use fabrics made of man-made fibres for patchwork but you will find that the turnings do not crease as well as cotton. Watch iron settings when pressing these fabrics.

Tools and equipment
All of the things you need are basic sewing equipment. Basting thread is quite important. You will use a lot of it so get a large reel. You will also need a quantity of pins. Choose the glass-headed dressmaker type. These are very thin and sharp and the best kind for patchwork.
Sewing threads Mercerized cotton thread should be used for cotton fabrics, No. 100 if you can handle it. Use pure silk thread for silk patchwork and a synthetic thread for materials made from man-made fibres. Match colours to the fabrics whenever you can but if you are limited to only one or two thread colours, use black with dark-coloured fabrics and white with light fabrics.
Needles should be as fine a gauge as you can manage.
Have at least two pairs of scissors. One pair should be kept for cutting backing papers. Make sure you know which pair is which because once scissors have been used for paper, they are not much good for anything else.
Paper for backings The paper backings which are used for mounting patches should be crisp and firm yet not too thick. Old gift cards are ideal and so is brown wrapping paper.
Templates Template is another word for 'pattern' and in patchwork, templates are used for cutting out the fabric shapes.
Templates are usually made of metal or plastic and are sold commercially in packs of two. The smaller template in the pack is opaque and is used for cutting the backing papers. The larger is made of transparent plastic and has a frosted border. This template is used for cutting fabrics and because it is transparent, you can choose just the area of pattern you want.
The patchwork shapes which are most popular are the pentagon, the hexagon and the octagon. The hexagon is called 'the beginner's patch' because it is versatile and is the easiest to work with. Other shapes are the long hexagon, the long diamond, the lozenge diamond,

the coffin lid, the church window and the clamshell. There are also templates for squares, rectangles and triangles.

Other equipment
To make the projects in this book, you will also need some squared, dressmakers' paper, tracing paper, stiff card for appliqué templates. You will need hard pencils, soft pencils, a ruler, a tape measure, a set square and some dressmakers' chalk in pencil form.

The basic techniques
There are two basic techniques in patchwork. The method originated by the settler women is called 'piecing' and the designs are based on geometric shapes arranged in blocks. The blocks are repeated and are joined together with strips and borders to make a complete quilt. Piecing is worked by joining pieces of fabric with running stitches. Nowadays, piecing is often done with a sewing machine for quickness. In fact, very little of the beauty of the patterns is lost in machine stitching because the charm of American patchwork lies in the colours and the way in which the shapes are put together. Traditional patchwork on the other hand relies entirely on hand sewing and the neatness of the work.

Traditional patchwork The effect of traditional patchwork is more formal – rather like a mosaic of fabric. The patches can be much smaller than in piecing and they are joined together with oversewing stitches. The fabric pieces are mounted on backing papers cut from a template and careful stitching is essential for a good finished effect.

Finishing patchwork
When all the patches have been joined, press it under a dry cloth and then clip the basting stitches and shake the papers out. The papers can be used again but should be discarded once they lose their crispness. Household items can be lined with calico. Quilts are generally lined with new cotton sheeting. Garments made of patchwork are lined with lightweight cotton or ordinary lining fabric.

Owl in appliqué

Materials, tools and equipment
Felt, white and yellow, beige, black
Red felt for the background
Piece of hardboard or cardboard for a base
Stranded embroidery threads, blue, black
Needle, pins, tracing paper, pencil
Scissors, clear strong adhesive

Method
Draw your owl first. Keep the outline simple **(1)**. Trace the design and then cut the various parts of the owl into pieces to make patterns **(2)**. Pin the paper patterns to felt and cut them out **(3)**. Embroider any details you want on the pieces at this stage. The owl illustrated has feather stitch on his wings **(4)** and big running stitches round his eyes **(5)**. Cross stitches and straight stitches have also been used by the designer, but you should decide for yourself which stitches will produce the best effect on your owl. Pin and then baste all the pieces to the background fabric placing the eyes, wing, feet pieces etc in position **(6)**. Work blanket stitch or buttonhole stitch round all the edges.
To mount the appliqué picture, cut the hardboard or cardboard 50mm (2in) smaller all round than the picture. Place the picture face down on the table and lay the board on top. Mark and then cut off the corners diagonally. Fold the sides of the picture onto the board and glue down. The picture is now ready for framing **(7)**.

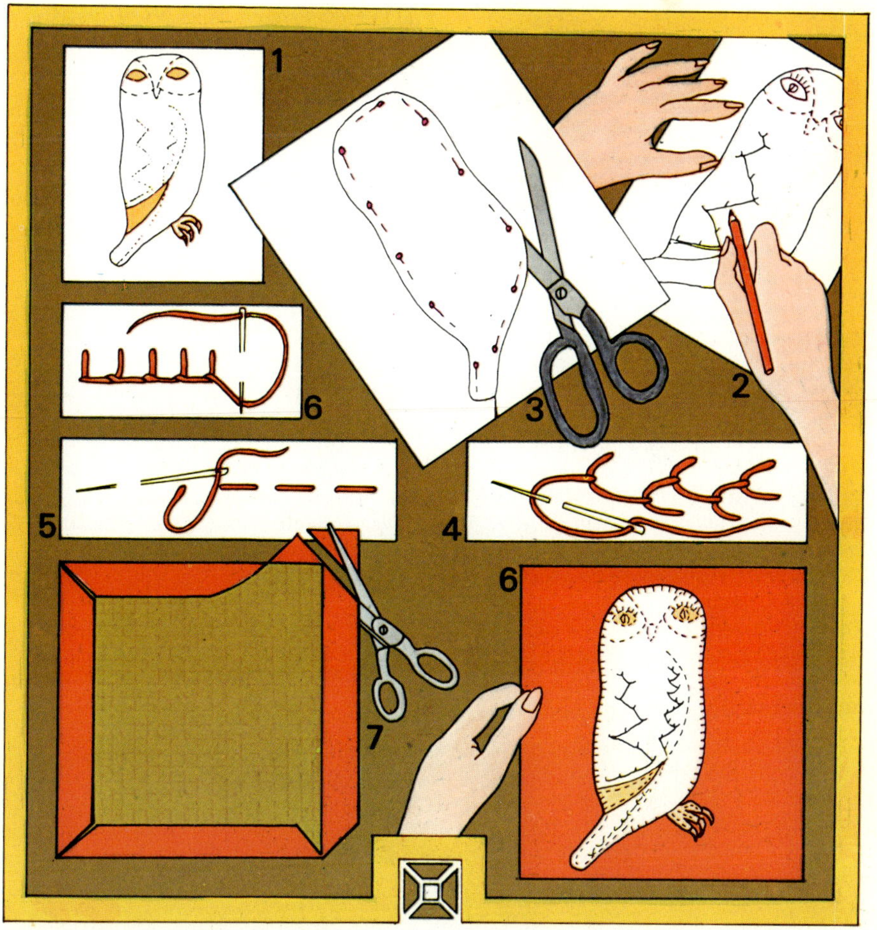

Appliqué is the art of sewing fabric shapes onto a background to make up a picture or a design. There are different ways of doing appliqué, depending on the fabric being used and the eventual use of the item. Clothes and household furnishings, which are likely to get a lot of wear and washing, must have the appliqué very firmly stitched down so that the edges do not fray. Very simple fabric shapes can be stitched down with zigzag machine stitching. Appliqué designs with small pieces of fabric and more complicated shapes must be sewn by hand with small stitches. Appliqué pictures need not have the pieces sewn down very securely so embroidery stitches can be used to do the job of holding the pieces in position and making a decoration at the same time. There are no hard and fast rules about making appliqué pictures: some of the pieces can be glued down without sewing if this seems to help the design; beads, buttons, threads etc., can be glued on or stitched on, just as the designer feels is best and most effective.

The owl picture was worked by a 10-year-old boy and was his first appliqué project. His mother liked it so much she framed it and it hangs on her living room wall. Perhaps you can make an appliqué picture for someone?

Fruit on denim

Appliqué can be as simple or as complex a design as you like but to begin, choose simple shapes which are easy to handle and sew. The fruit design is made up of several very simple shapes which are stitched down separately, some overlapping others. The technique described is the traditional appliqué method used by the early American pioneer women in the making of their pieced patchwork quilts which often included blocks of appliqué.
If preferred, the fruit design can be worked in machine appliqué (see pages 12–13).

Materials, tools and equipment
Scraps of plain coloured fabrics, yellow, orange, green, red and brown
Matching sewing threads, needle, Vilene (Pellon), card for templates, squared paper, carbon paper
Scissors, soft pencil
Stranded embroidery threads, green, black, yellow, brown, embroidery needle

Method
Draw the graph pattern up to size on squared paper. The scale is 1 square to 20mm (¾in) **(1)**. Transfer the enlarged pattern pieces onto card to make templates. Cut out the templates **(2)**. Hold a template down on fabric. Draw round outline lightly in pencil **(3)**. Cut out the shape with 9mm (⅜in) extra all round for turnings. Snip into the turnings on curves **(4)**. Using the same templates, cut out the shapes in Vilene. Lay the Vilene shapes on the wrong side of the fabric shapes and iron the turnings to the wrong side **(5)**. Arrange the prepared appliqué pieces on the back-

ground fabric. Note which overlap. Baste them in position **(6)**. The appliqué is stitched to the background with tiny hemming stitches using a closely matching thread **(7)**.
Work embroidery details on the fruit. The line on the banana is worked in stem stitch in brown thread. The lemon detail and the green leaf outline on the apple are also in stem stitch. The black calyx on the orange is 4 chain stitches worked to make a lazy daisy **(8)**.
Note Appliqué is usually worked without the need for backing, but using Vilene behind the shapes helps a beginner to get a clean edge when pressing the turnings. As you become more experienced, you will be able to fold the turnings neatly and accurately with a finger and thumb as you hem.

Alphabet bedcover

Machine appliqué is quick to do and is the best technique for items which are going to get a lot of wear or be laundered often.

Many quilt-makers use machine appliqué and the result is certainly hardwearing.

There are two techniques, both very similar. The method described for making the alphabet quilt is used when there are several shapes making a design or pattern. The second method can be used for single appliqué shapes.

Method 1

Plan the quilt on squared paper to decide how big the squares are going to be and how many you will have across the quilt and down. The quilt illustrated is for a child's bed and the squares were 200mm (8in) with 110mm (4½in) letters. Cut the background squares of fabric with 12mm (½in) extra all round for seams.

Design the letters and numbers for the appliqué, working on squared paper. Plan the fabrics you will use for them to get the best contrast.

Trace the letters and numbers and transfer each one onto cardboard or onto the back of fine sandpaper to make templates.

Lay the appliqué fabric on the table top right side up and place the template in position. Draw round the outline with a soft, sharp pencil **(1)**. Use the same template to draw the outline of the letter on the background fabric **(2)**. Lay the cut-out letter right side down and spread fabric adhesive on the back. Do

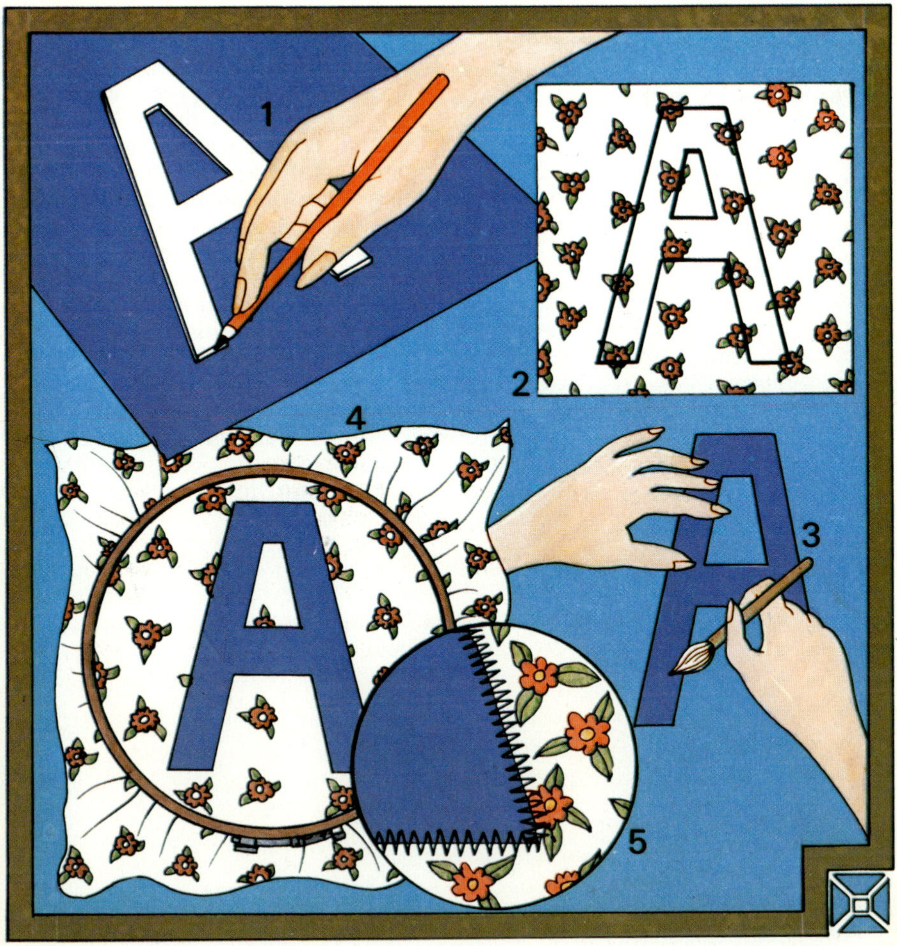

not use too much or the glue will seep through and spoil the fabric **(3)**. Fabric adhesive cannot be washed out or removed in any way. Leave the adhesive to get tacky and then press the letter down onto the background fabric. Smooth it to remove creases. Put the fabric square into an embroidery ring – this helps to keep the fabric taut while machining. Set the machine to a zigzag 1½–2 and to a medium stitch length. Zigzag stitch round the appliqué covering the raw edges **(4) (5)**.

To make up the quilt, join the squares in strips and then join the strips. Back the quilt with a piece of plain fabric.

Method 2 Draw out the letter or shape on the fabric. Cut out with at least 25mm (1in) extra all round. Place the cutout on the background fabric and baste it in position. Machine stitch on the pencilled line (ordinary machine stitching) or work tiny running stitches by hand. Trim the excess fabric back almost to the stitching line. Work zigzag stitch over the stitching, making sure that the zigzag stitch is wide enough to go into the appliqué on one side of the stitching line and goes just past the line into the background fabric on the other. The appliqué shape will be very securely stitched to the background.

Working in squares

Patchwork joined up with running stitches is termed 'American patchwork' because this was the method used by the American pioneer women three hundred years ago. Today, the same patterns can be stitched using a sewing machine. The effect is not quite the same but it is much quicker and whole quilts can be stitched in just a month or two. Hand-sewn quilts sometimes took the pioneer women more than a year to complete! The technique described is for the traditional method – hand sewing – but you can use a sewing machine if you prefer.

The square is a good shape for beginners. It is easy to cut out, it can be sewn by hand or by machine and it joins up quicker than any other shape. Squares patchwork is very versatile. You can use it for so many things – quilts – such as the beautiful blue quilt illustrated – curtains, tea cosies, cushions, table mats, as well as for smart clothes. Skirts, blouses – even dresses – look marvellous in patchwork worked in squares. The squares can be any size from about 50mm (2in) to 150mm (6in) depending on what you are making.

Making a template Your patchwork will be easier to do and better finished if the fabric pieces are accurately cut. The shapes in American patchwork are geometric and you can cut the templates yourself. Use a ruler and a set square for accuracy. The template can be made of stiff card or heavy notepaper but the best material is fine sandpaper. This has the advantage that

when it is placed rough side down on fabric, it does not slip about while you are drawing round. Only one template is required. All the fabric pieces are cut from the same template, but of course you should make a new one if the edges become damaged or broken.

Measure and cut out the template. Iron the fabrics smooth. Lay them right side down on a flat surface with the grain of the fabric (the weave) lying straight. Place the template on the fabric and, with a soft pencil, draw round **(1)**. Move the template about 12mm (½in) away and draw round again. Be careful not to stretch or pull the fabric. This pencilled line will be your sewing line. Cut out the squares, allowing 6mm (¼in) all round from the line.

Sewing patches together The patches are sewn together with small running stitches **(2)**. Start and end with a back stitch. Join squares into strips and then sew strips together. Press all seams open on the wrong side as you work **(3)**.

When the patchwork is finished, it can be left just as it is and used for a quilt, cushion cover or tablecloth, etc., or it can be further embellished with stitching. You can work machine zigzag stitches along the seams **(4)**, or work topstitching along the sides of the seams **(5)**.

There are different ways of making and finishing quilts. The blue quilt illustrated was mounted on a backing, wrong sides together, the edges turned under and topstitched all round **(6)**.

Geometric patterns

Once you have successfully pieced squares, experiment with patterns using squares and rectangles for more informal effects. Cut rectangles to the same width as squares and seam them into strips, mixing them. Join the strips in random colour schemes **(1)**. Cut a large square and set smaller squares and rectangles round it for a block pattern **(2)**. Using rectangles only, make a 'brick wall pattern'. This looks effective if some of the fabrics are plain and the patterned patches are grouped in one area **(3)**.
Arrange rectangles in a woven pattern – rather like parquet flooring **(4)**.

Squares and triangles
Squares can be divided diagonally to make 2-patch blocks and 4-patch blocks **(5)**. Triangles based on squares form the basis of dozens of different block designs.

1–5 this page reading from top to bottom.

Double X uses big and small triangles and squares **(6)**.
The Pierced Star is striking in its effect. Cut triangles and rhomboids **(7)**.
Flight of Bees is a famous pattern. Use 3 different fabrics for the best effect **(8)**.
Cats and Mice looks most effective when squares of plain colour are set between the arms of the cross. This design is deceptively simple. 5 squares and 16 small triangles make the pattern and 4 large half-squares complete the block **(9)**.

Flight of Birds is a pattern made up with triangles of different sizes **(10)**.
Pinwheel is a complex-looking pattern, all in triangles **(11)**.
Greek Cross can be used to make a superb geometric-patterned quilt. Join the blocks in different arrangements, so that the bold red band makes a distinctive pattern **(12)**.
By studying these block patterns, you begin to see how triangles and squares can be used to get all kinds of effects. Blocks 6, 7, and 11 are obviously 4-block patterns – that is, the basic

square has been divided into 4, then the quarters divided again into four. The other variation is 9-block patterns. Block 9, Cats and Mice is a 9-block pattern. With these two basic block formations, you can begin to design your own patchwork patterns.

6–12 this page reading from top left to bottom right.

Designing a quilt

Decide the colour scheme of your quilt and then decide upon the size. Many of the traditional patchwork quilts are designed in blocks about 30cm (12in) square and the block is repeated all over the quilt with perhaps a different block motif in the centre. Draw the dimensions of your quilt on squared paper. Decide on a workable scale.
On 10mm (⅜in) squares you might decide, for instance, on a scale of 1 square to 150mm (6in). Work out the size of a block which would fit the length and width of the quilt. If you have to add a little to the measurements to make a square fit, do so.
Now you are ready to design the repeat block. Draw the block to a larger scale below the quilt plan. Arrange in front of you the fabrics you are planning to use and number them. Design the block pattern using simple geometric shapes (see page 17 for ideas). Number the different colours so that you know which fabrics are being used where. Now you know how many patches have to be cut from each fabric to make a block, and by multiplying the number of blocks on the plan, how many you need for the whole quilt.

The next stage is to make the templates

Only one template is used to cut all the patches of the same shape. Working to scale, draw up each of the geometric shapes in the block to life size. Then cut each shape out of fine sandpaper.

The blue and white patchwork pattern illustrated is a detail from an antique American quilt. The pattern is called 'Blue Wrench' and is a good example of the way designs can be made using just two geometric shapes. Blue Wrench uses only triangles and squares of different sizes **(1)**. It is a unique design because the blue patches are cleverly arranged on a white ground in such a way that the wrench design is repeated in white.
Although there are no tricky corners to sew in this pattern, because the designer has broken the design down into quite small pieces, it is sometimes unavoidable. Patterns which use large triangles of different colours are better worked by setting the triangles into a triangular-shaped space.

Setting a triangle To sew a triangle into a triangular space, seam up to the corner and fasten off the thread. Then seam towards the corner from the other side of the triangle **(2)**. You can either clip into the corner or press the seam flat. If it is necessary to join three pieces into a corner, seam two pieces but stop stitching just at the point where the seams of the third piece will begin. Fasten off the thread ends. Stitch the two sides of the third piece towards the corner, stopping when the seam lines meet **(3)**. If the patches are large enough, use hand sewing or sewing machine, as you prefer **(4)**.
Making your own patterns It is fun to see if you can make a picture in geometric shapes **(5):** butterflies, trees, flowers, houses or animals.

Chevron quilt

This brilliant quilted bedcover is a modern interpretation of the traditional American pieced quilt. Only one geometric shape is used – the rhomboid (an equilateral but not right-angled lozenge diamond). The triangle which completes the strips at the end is half of a rhomboid.

Four fabrics are used, three plain colours, yellow, pale orange and deep orange plus a spotted scarlet. The scarlet fabric is used as a border to 'frame' the chevron design of the pieced work.

Materials, tools and equipment

Four fabrics to the colour scheme
Sheeting to the finished quilt size for backing
Graph paper, card or fine sandpaper for templates, scissors, pins, needle, thread, sewing machine (optional)
Terylene wadding (medium weight), long needle, basting thread

Method

Plan the design of the quilt on squared paper (pages 18–19) **(1)** and draw an accurate rhomboid. Cut out the rhomboid template and draw round it on the wrong side of the fabric **(2)**. Cut out all the fabric pieces for the quilt with 9mm (⅜in) seam allowance all round. Use the pencil line as a stitching line. Stitch pieces together with running stitches or machine stitching and make up strips **(3)**. Join strips following your colour plan **(4)**. Cut a template in half to make triangles for the ends of the strips **(5)**. Join strips to make up the quilt **(6)**.

Spread the completed quilt top on the

floor and measure it. Cut the backing to the same size plus 25mm (1in) all round. Prepare the Terylene wadding. This is usually sold in narrow strips and it is necessary to join strips to get sufficient width for a large quilt. Join strips with loop stitches (rather like a large blanket stitch). Spread the backing on the floor (or table) wrong side of fabric up, and make sure that it is lying absolutely square and smooth. Lift the Terylene wadding and spread it on the backing sheet. Keep both layers as smooth as possible. The next stage is rather difficult to do alone. Try to get someone to help. Lay the quilt top on the wadding and smooth it out.

Basting This is a long, tiring job but essential for achieving a good finish. Thread a long needle with basting thread and work 25mm (1in) long basting stitches through all thicknesses. Start in the centre and baste to the sides. Then baste from the centre to the top and the bottom.

Baste the entire quilt, working a squared grid of stitches. You will need to wear a thimble because pushing through all the layers is hard on the middle finger! The quilt is now ready for quilting. (Pages 22–23.)

Quilting

Very few modern homes have sufficient space for a quilting frame, and machine quilting has taken the place of the beautiful handwork.

Quilting designs After the 3 layers of the quilt have been basted together **(1)** the quilting design is marked on the surface. The simplest quilting patterns are straight lines in diamonds or squares or following the seam lines of the quilt. The detail from the quilt illustrated shows hand quilting worked diagonally across the green and white squares, outlining the motif and in a decorative flower design. Traditional quilting designs include fruit, flowers, fans, shells, stars, feathers and other decorative shapes.

Marking quilting lines There are different methods of marking the quilting lines. In the traditional method, the point of a darning needle is used to mark round a template. The needle makes a mark which can be easily seen. Some needlewomen mark quilting lines with dressmaker's chalk because this can be brushed off the work afterwards. Pencil should never be used because it cannot be removed. Pouncing, a technique used in surface embroidery for marking patterns, works very well. Draw the quilting design on tracing paper. Prick holes along the pencil lines. Powder some chalk. Roll up a strip of blotting paper to make a stub. Hold the tracing over the quilt and dab chalk through the holes **(2)**.

Machine quilting Fit a No. 11 (Continental No. 80) needle to the machine, plus the embroidery foot, and cover the feed dog with the plate provided for the purpose. Thread up the machine and the bobbin with nylon thread. (Nylon thread cannot be ironed – but quilted covers should never be ironed any-

way.) Set the stitch length to between 2½–3. Roll the quilt tightly and fit it under the arm of the machine, right side up **(3)**. Stitch with a smooth working action – this produces a better effect. The covered feed dog means that you must pull the quilt gently under the needle.

Hand quilting If quilts are formed in blocks, these can be hand-quilted before being stitched together. A large embroidery frame is recommended because this makes the work easier. Mount the patchwork on top of the wadding and backing in the usual way, and baste to hold all three layers together. Place the block in a frame. Rest the edge of the frame against the table. Make a small knot in the end of the thread. Insert the thread from underneath and pull the knot gently into the wadding. Work running stitches along the quilting lines, about 9 to 25mm (1in) passing the needle from the hand above the work to the hand below and then back up through the quilting. Do not quilt right up to the edges of the block. Leave about 9mm (⅜in) unstitched all round **(5)**.

To join quilted blocks, separate the layers at the edges. Place two blocks together, right sides facing. Stitch through the seam allowance of the patchwork. Turn the blocks face down. Fold one edge of the backing under, place it over the opposite edge and hem the two together. Join all the blocks in the same way.

Quilting was traditionally done by hand with the work set on a frame **(4)**.

Oakleaf quilt

The Oakleaf quilt is based on an old American pieced quilt design called Whig Rose but the motif makes a very good appliqué design for a block or for a smaller item such as a cushion.

Materials, tools and equipment
White foundation cotton fabric
Red, yellow, green cotton fabrics for appliqué
Needles, threads
Graph paper, pencil, fine sandpaper

Method
If you are making a quilt, plan the arrangement of the blocks first **(1)**. Cut the foundation squares 415mm × 415mm (16in × 16in) in white fabric. Draw up the graph pattern to life size. The scale is 1 square to 10mm (7⁄16in). Trace the shapes on to the back of fine sandpaper to make templates **(2)**. Cut out the appliqué pieces. Prepare and stitch them to the foundation square (see page 10) **(3)**. Make up enough blocks for the quilt. Cut the strips and squares for joining blocks. The red strips are about 430mm × 62mm (17in × 2½in). The small yellow pieces are 62mm (2½in) square.
Join two blocks to each side of a red strip. Stitch a yellow square to one end of the strip. Join two more blocks and two more strips **(4)**. Continue to join blocks and strips. Cut 415mm (16in) squares of green fabric, and cut them in half diagonally to make the filling triangles for the sides of the quilt. The quilt illustrated is bound with red fabric to finish the edges **(5)**.

Friendship Quilts

A charming American tradition which is worth copying today was the making of Friendship quilts. 300 years ago, a girl would be expected to have made 12 quilts for her Hope Chest before she got engaged to be married. The Friendship quilt was the 13th quilt and quite different. Once a girl was engaged, her friends got together to make appliqué pictures for a quilt. Sometimes the pictures were scenes from the bride's life, but often they were just something which the maker thought attractive and interesting.
Houses, horses, flower sprays, moon and stars, birds, trees – anything that made a colourful and pretty block of appliqué was stitched – and, on a given day, the blocks were brought to a party to be 'set'. The friends worked their names or initials on the blocks and then the blocks were joined with strips of calico or pieced patchwork. Later still, the friends came again to a 'quilting bee', when the Friendship quilt was backed and quilted ready for the bride's first home.

Pentagon ball and a pig

This first project in traditional patchwork uses the five-sided pentagon.

Materials, tools and equipment
Felt pieces of different colours
Terylene filling or cotton wool
Pentagon template
Pencil, scissors, needle, threads

Method
Cut 12 pentagons from felt **(1)**. Separate them into two heaps of 6. Choose one patch for the centre and then arrange the other five round it as a 'flower'. Pick up the centre patch and one other patch and sew them together. To do this, hold the two patches together, corners and edges exactly matching. Pin them together if it helps. Thread the needle with a thread which is the same as the darkest colour. Lay the end of the thread along the top of the two patches so that you are ready to start sewing from the right hand end. Start making small upright oversewing stitches, the first stitches lying over the thread end. If you do it this way, you will be getting into a good sewing habit. Knots are never used on

the end of thread in good patchwork. When you get to the end of the seam, you can either immediately start on the next patch or finish off the seam with two or three oversewing stitches. Sew all the patches round the centre patch in the same way **(2)**. Now the flower shape is closed up into a half ball by joining the side seams of the five pentagons. With the remaining six patches, make another half-ball. If you now hold the two half-balls together you will see that the points of one neatly fit into the spaces between the points of the other. Making sure that you are still sewing on the same side of the felt, join the halves with oversewing **(3)**. One point must be left unstitched so that there is a hole for turning the ball right side out and for filling.

Turn the ball and fill it through the hole, pushing the filling down with a pencil. Lastly, close up the hole with oversewing **(4)**.

Making a pig. The ball was made with oversewing. The pig is made in the same way but has one patch sewn in with running stitches. Cut 12 pink pentagons and sew six together to make a half-ball. Then sew five together, four round one, leaving one patch out for the pig's face **(5)**. Fill the ball and leave it aside while you make the pig's face. Cut three small circles of pink felt and sew them together to the face for a snub nose **(6)**. Cut two small circles of black felt for eyes. Sew them to the face **(7)**. Now sew the face patch into the body using running stitches **(8)**. The ears of the pig illustrated are made of proper, double-sided fabric patches. You can try this later when you have become more experienced with patchwork. Give your pig two ears made of felt, stitching them to the seams above the eyes **(9)**. To make the four stumpy feet, cut 100mm × 12mm (4in × ½in) strips of black felt. Roll up and oversew the seam. Stitch the feet under the body **(10)**. Make a tail of felt or wool yarn.

Hexagons

A hexagon shape is given **(1)** which you can trace off and use to make cardboard templates. The outer hexagon is for cutting fabric and the inner for cutting papers. Trace them off carefully and then transfer them onto thin stiff cardboard using typist's carbon paper. Cut out both templates using sharp scissors.

Cutting backing papers
Backing papers are used behind the fabric patch to make clean, sharp edges while the patches are being stitched together. Postcards, stiff note-paper, brown wrapping paper etc., make good backing papers. Lay the small template on the paper and draw round with a sharpened pencil. Cut out on the pencilled line carefully **(2)**. It is very important that papers are accurately cut because they determine the shape of the finished patch.

Cutting fabric patches
Hold the larger template on the fabric and pencil round. Cut out the patch on the pencilled line **(3)**.

Mounting patches Pin the paper to the wrong side of the patch. Fold the turnings onto the paper and pin all six sides **(4)**. Thread a needle with basting thread and tie a knot in the end. Baste all round the patch to hold it to the paper, making a pleat in the fabric at the corners.
Hold each pleat with one basting stitch **(5)**. Remove the pins as you work. When you are more experienced you will be able to baste the turnings with-

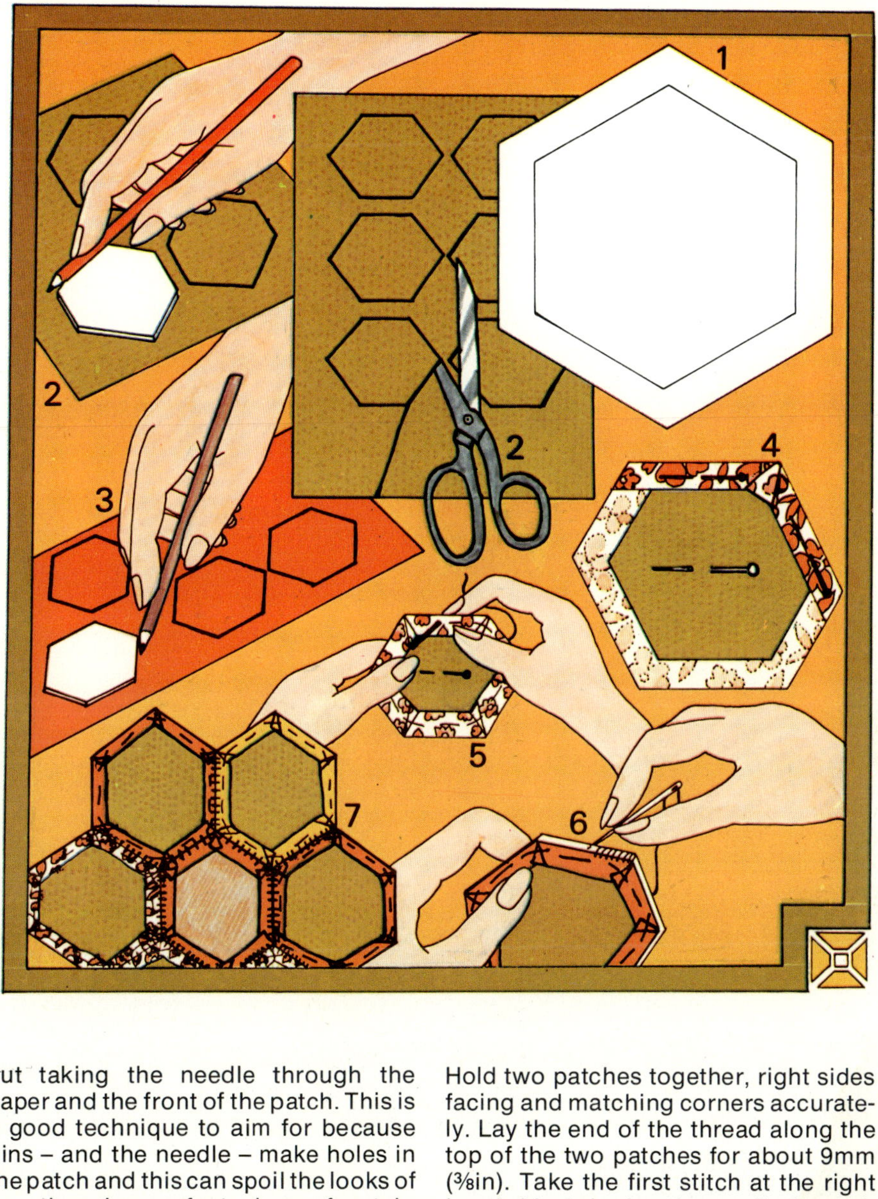

out taking the needle through the paper and the front of the patch. This is a good technique to aim for because pins – and the needle – make holes in the patch and this can spoil the looks of an otherwise perfect piece of patchwork. For the moment, however, baste right through the paper and the fabric patch to hold them together.

Sewing patches together
The stitch that is used to sew patchwork is oversewing and the stitches must be small and upright. Thread the needle with a matching sewing thread. Hold two patches together, right sides facing and matching corners accurately. Lay the end of the thread along the top of the two patches for about 9mm (⅜in). Take the first stitch at the right hand side, bringing the needle through from the back. Work the oversewing stitches through the edges of the fabric only (try not to pick up the papers), and work the stitches over the laid thread to secure the end **(6)**. Knots are not used in good patchwork. You can finish off at the end of the seam with a double stitch or you can start joining a new patch **(7)**.

Designing with fabrics

Hexagons have been called the beginner's patch because, not only are they the easiest of the shapes to sew together, but they are so versatile in pattern building. Hexagons alone can be used to make beautiful patterns and colour effects without using other shapes. They can be used in a random way, mixing colours, textures and fabrics – as in the closeup of the quilt – or they can be stitched into rosettes and double rosettes and used as flowers or star shapes.

Ideas for hexagons
Six hexagons set round a single hexagon makes a rosette. By using a plain fabric for the central hexagon and a patterned or flowered fabric for the six surrounding hexagons, a motif very like a flower is produced. There is a very famous patchwork pattern called Grandmother's Garden which uses rosettes in just this way. The central hexagon is usually yellow or orange, and flowered patterns are used for the first round of patches. Another round of hexagons is added – usually in green fabric – to suggest foliage. The double rosettes thus formed are joined together with cream or white calico patches to represent twisting garden paths. The finished effect is very pretty, and making a quilt in this pattern is a very good group project because friends can work on rosettes and join them up into a quilt later.

A very colourful effect can be made by making up 7 rosettes in different fabrics but with a strong colour scheme in one of them. Set this rosette as the central motif and group the remaining rosettes round it. Join the 7 rosettes to other rosettes with a plain, light-coloured fabric. All the rosettes should have the one with a strong colour scheme as a central motif which gives the finished patchwork an overall planned look. The effect is of enormous flowers grouped together.

Designing with fabrics

If patterned fabrics are cleverly used with hexagons, very striking effects can be achieved. Use the window template to cut certain areas and arrange the hexagons to see what new patterns evolve. You will be surprised how the fabric motif changes once six are grouped together. Choose a section of a stripe for instance **(1)** and use it vertically. It would look quite different used horizontally. Also, hexagons cut from a richly-flowered fabric and set into garlands across a plain fabric look amazingly like a piece of fabric printed with groups of flowers. This idea would make a beautiful edging for a patchwork skirt or for a cushion pattern.

Fabrics and other shapes

Hexagons and diamonds work well together in patchwork, and it is worth while trying the effects of patterned fabrics in stars made of diamonds, combining them with hexagon flowers. Stripes look very striking **(2)** and you might like to experiment with striped diamond stars combined with plain fabric hexagon rosettes with a striped centre. Or a patterned fabric for the star so that it looks like a flower against a background of plain hexagons **(3)**.

PROJECT

Two tortoise toys

The two tortoises are made in the same way. The outer line on the hexagon and the head, tail and feet shapes are for making the mother tortoise. The inner line makes the pieces for the smaller baby.

Materials, tools and equipment

Flowered and plain fabrics, about 250mm (10in)
Felt to tone with fabric colours
Filling, needle, thread
Pins, tracing paper, scissors, soft pencil
Stiff card, backing paper
Pair of googlie eyes for each tortoise

Method

Trace the hexagon shape and transfer it carefully onto card to make a template. Cut it out. Cut 14 backing papers **(1)**. Use the same template to cut the fabric patches. Lay the template on the wrong side of the fabric and draw round. Cut out 9mm (⅜in) larger all round. Cut 12 patches from the patterned fabric and 2 from the plain. Mount the patches and join 6 flowered patches round a plain patch to make a 'rosette' **(2)**. Make up another rosette in the same way. Press carefully and remove the papers.

Head, tail and feet Trace the shapes and cut up the tracing for patterns. Cut 2 head pieces, 2 tails and 8 feet from felt. Sew 2 heads together with over-

sewing leaving straight end open for filling **(3)**. Sew 2 tails together and the feet in pairs to make 4 feet. Stuff lightly and oversew the ends closed. Lay one of the rosettes right side up on the table. Place the head, tail and feet in position in the angles, the straight edge of the felt pieces to the outside of the rosette. Pin and baste **(4)**. Lay the second rosette on top, right side down, matching the points and angles and sandwiching the felt pieces. Baste and stitch round on the seam line of the hexagon patches **(5)**, but leave one side of a hexagon open for turning to right side. Remove the basting, trim the seam allowance and turn the tortoise right side out. Press lightly. Fill so that the tortoise is firm but not hard, and close the open seam with neat oversewing. Sew or glue on the googlie eyes **(6)**.

Pincushions in patchwork
The basic shape of the tortoises, a rosette made up of seven hexagons, makes a good pincushion. The cushion should be filled rather more firmly and sawdust can be used if preferred. A dressmaker will appreciate a small pincushion stitched to a wrist band so that she can wear it as she works.

Work bag

The girl who made the patchwork for this workbag did it as a hand sewing project in needlework class but, when she started, she had no idea what the patchwork would make when it was finished. Luckily, she worked a rectangle and it was easy to turn it into a workbag. It is much better to have a shape in mind when you start doing patchwork or you may simply waste time – and patchwork.

Materials, tools and equipment
Cotton fabrics for patchwork, medium weight
Vilene (Pellon) for interlining for bag, 45cm (½yd) of lining fabric
Pair of wooden bag handles, 330mm (13½in approx) wide
Hexagon templates [sides 25mm (1in)]
Ruler, squared graph paper, soft pencil or chalk pencil, needles, pins, basting thread, sewing thread, scissors, black embroidery cotton

Method
Start by drawing up the pattern for the bag from the graph pattern. The scale is 1 square to 40mm (1⅝in). You will use the pattern shape for cutting out the front and back of the bag, the Vilene interlining and the lining itself **(1)**. Make enough patchwork for the front and back of the bag. If you decide to have patchwork on the front only, you will need some fabric for the back **(2)**. Press the completed patchwork and remove the papers. Cut 2 pieces of Vilene (Pellon) to the shape and baste the patchwork front and Vilene together. Baste Vilene (Pellon) to the back piece too. Cut out the paper pattern. Pin it to the Vilene (Pellon) side and, using a

chalk pencil, draw round the outline. Do the same on the bag back **(3)**. Cut out both 12mm (½in) away from the pencilled line. The pencilled line is the seam line on which you will stitch the bag together. Mark the big dots on each side of the bag. This is where the gusset opening begins. Now pin the paper pattern to the doubled lining fabric. Draw round the pattern. Cut out the linings 12mm (½in) away from the line. You are now ready to sew the bag together. Pin and baste the two linings together, right sides facing, and then stitch from one dot to the other, leaving the straight top of the bag open **(4)**. Remove basting. Now pin and baste the two interlining-backed bag pieces together, patchwork and backing facing. Sew all round from dot to dot. Trim the seam allowance of both bag and lining to about half for a neat seam. Turn the bag to the right side and press. Put the lining inside the bag. Fold under the seam allowance on the top edges of both bag and lining. Pin and baste. Oversew the two edges together **(5)**. Lay the bag, patchwork side up, on the table and place one of the handles on the inside of the bag, the holes just below the edge. Thread a needle with embroidery cotton. Tie a knot in the thread end. Take a small stitch in the lining and bring the needle through the first hole. Take it through to the back through the next adjacent hole. Bring the needle back through the same hole about 3mm (⅛in) along. Continue and then sew the other handle in the same way **(6)**.

Make a simple cushion

When you have made your piece of patchwork, you will want to turn it into a cushion. Here is how it is done.

Materials, tools and equipment
Finished patchwork for the cushion front, cushion pad
Matching fabric for the back
Needle, thread, scissors
Sewing machine (optional)
Matching silk cord for edging

Method
Press the finished patchwork and remove the backing papers. Cut the backing fabric to exactly the same size. Place the two sides of the cushion together, right sides facing, matching the corners. Pin and baste them together 12mm (½in) from the edge. Remove the pins. Set the sewing machine to a medium-sized stitch and sew on the seam line, pivoting the needle at the corners. Start stitching in the middle of a side and stop about 100mm (4in) away from where you started **(6)**.
Make sure that you start and finish by either running the machine backwards and forwards or knotting off the ends securely. If you are sewing your cushion by hand, use backstitches **(5)**.
Press open the seam and then press it flat again. Cut into the corners almost to the stitches. This is so that the corners are sharp. Turn the cushion to the right side. Trim some of the seam allowance away at the corners. Put in the cushion pad and close the seam with tiny oversewing stitches. Stitch on the cord with hemming stitches, twisting the cord into a loop at the corners.

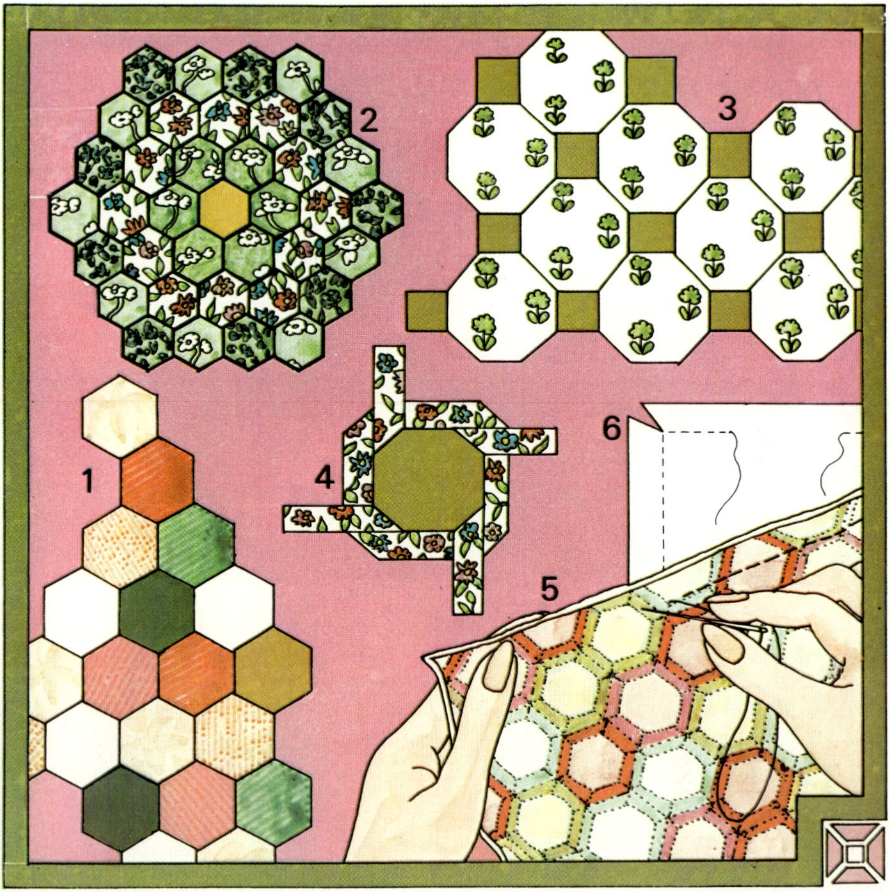

Octagons

Cushions are very good patchwork projects because they do not take very long to make, and they are always useful for gifts. Three different approaches are illustrated. The cushion in the centre is made of silk fabrics which glisten, and strong colours have been chosen to contrast with pale tones. Here the hexagons are used in a random pattern, but the finished effect is striking because the colour scheme is good **(1)**. The cushion on the right uses hexagons in a different way. A triple rosette has been formed in closely related colours and patterns round a bright yellow patch. The rosette was then stitched to a background fabric with tiny, almost invisible stitches. The effect is of a patchwork cushion but appliqué has been used too **(2)**.

The octagon
The cushion on the left introduces a new patchwork shape – the octagon (8-sided shape). Octagons are easy to sew but it cannot be worked unless a square is used as well **(3)**. The designer has cleverly used a white fabric with a green motif and matched the square to the green. Note that the motif on the white fabric has been carefully placed so that every octagon is the same. Octagons can be used with bars and squares **(4)** and with squares, diamonds and church windows.

Tumbling blocks

The cushion illustrated is made up in a pattern called 'tumbling blocks'. It is a traditional American pattern but it is not often used for a whole quilt. The three-dimensional effect can be a bit jazzy on the eye and the pattern is best kept for smaller items, or used as a single block motif in a quilt.

Materials, tools and equipment
3 different fabrics of the same fibre (cotton, silk etc.,) in 3 tones
Diamond template
Backing paper, scissors, needle
Thread

Method
90 patches are used in the cushion cover illustrated but, as you build up the patchwork, papers can be removed from the central area and re-used. Cut about 40 papers – this should be enough. Cut 90 patches, 30 from each of the fabrics. Mount fabric on papers. Three patches make one block **(1)**. Sew three patches together **(2)** taking care to keep the fit of the points accurate. If diamond patches are badly joined there will be tiny holes between each patch. Join blocks of three together to make tumbling blocks pattern **(3)**. To finish the patchwork into a rectangle you will need two more templates. Cut one diamond template across the width and another along the length. Mount fabrics to complete the design. These shapes will fit into the sides of the patchwork **(4)**.

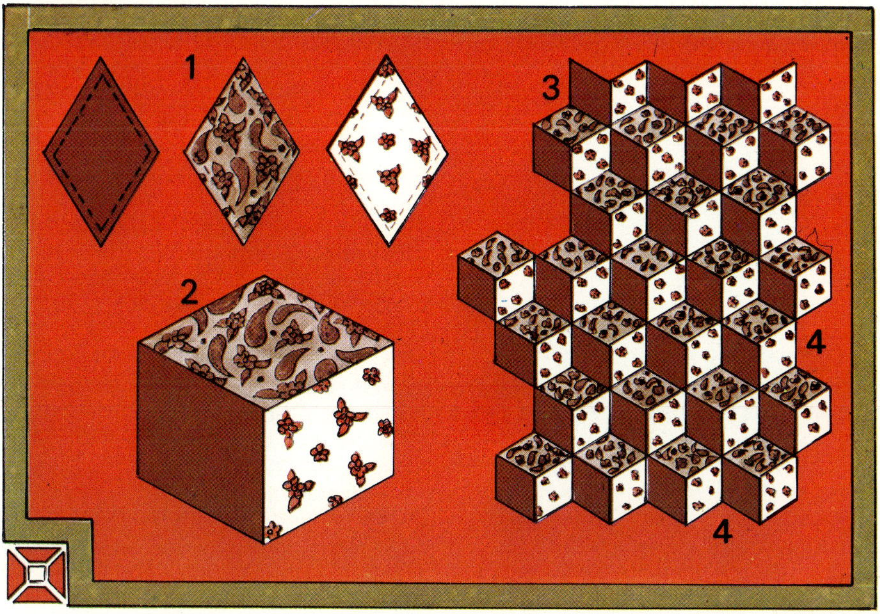

The diamond shape

Diamonds are versatile shapes and can be used in groups of 3, to make a cube effect (as illustrated), or in groups of 6 or 8 to make a star. They can be used with squares, hexagons and triangles providing the sides are the same length and the angles fit. Diamonds are often used to make border designs on quilts. There are two diamond shapes. One is the 'lozenge' and the other is narrower – the 'long diamond'.

Diamond patches are more difficult to mount than other shapes because the angles are narrower and the points sharper. The fabric has to be double folded and, folding and basting must be done with great care.

Mounting diamond patches

Cut out the fabric with one side of the template lying along the grain of the fabric. This prevents the patch from stretching too much as you work. Use very stiff card for the backing paper because this helps to keep the diamond's shape. Pin the backing paper to the fabric and fold the top right hand hem onto the paper first. Secure with two basting stitches. Fold down the point that is sticking up so that it lies on the top left hem. Fold the top left hand hem over. Baste to secure and then work on the two remaining sides of the diamond in the same way. By following this procedure, you will make neat, sharp points.

When stitching diamonds together, start sewing at the wider angled point first and work towards the narrow point.

This makes sure that the points are sharp and also that they fit together neatly which is very important if you are making a star motif.

Mounting triangles

Triangles made from squares have wide angles and are fairly easy to mount. Triangles that are half-diamonds have a short base line and longer sides. The angles are therefore more acute and the same technique as that used for mounting diamond patches is applied.

Patchwork appliqué

The panels of diamonds that go across the back, front and sleeves of the coat illustrated were made as a piece of patchwork, and then stitched to ordinary fabric before the coat was made up. The diamonds left an edge of points, so the designer cut diamonds in half to fill the spaces and thus achieved a straight edge.
You can get the effect of patchwork on your clothes even if they are already made or are shop bought by using a technique called 'patchwork appliqué'.
Patchwork appliqué involves making up pieces of patchwork, taking out the papers and then sewing the patchwork to another piece of fabric. It is a particularly pretty form of decoration and can be adapted to all kinds of things. The technique is very simple. To prevent the possibility of turnings showing through on the right side after the patchwork is mounted, cut the shape in muslin as well **(1)** and mount both fabric and muslin together **(2)**.
Stitch the patches together in the usual way, press carefully and remove the paper patches **(3)**. It is a good idea to baste the outside edges of a piece of patchwork before applying it. It helps to keep the edges in shape.

Ideas for appliqué patchwork
Appliqué patchwork can be used in a number of ways. Triangles, for instance, make very good edgings for handtowels, curtains, quilts etc. **(4)**, and they can also be used on skirt and

jacket hems or down the front of a jacket. Diamonds can be set on their long sides to make chevrons for an edging. This looks particularly effective in striped fabrics or stripes and solids. Squares and triangles make wide edgings, and so do triangles set like arrowheads touching. Each triangle is applied separately.

Hexagons are particularly useful for making appliqué decorations because they make rosettes and stars as well as forming neat edgings and bands. If small templates are used rosettes of hexagons can be used all over a tablecloth or curtains. Single rosettes look pretty on all kinds of household accessories, tea and coffee cosies, traycloths, cushions and tablemats **(5)**.

Try the effect of making rosettes of hexagons in brown and orange and mounting them into a plain, cream-coloured tablecloth as place settings. Make matching napkins in brown or orange with a tiny rosette in cream with a contrasting centre **(6)**.

Other patches make attractive appliqué motifs too. **Church windows** for instance, which are usually used with squares and diamonds, look marvellous set end to end as an edging for a skirt or a coat. You might use two rows and fill the square between them with a patch in a matching fabric **(7)**.

PROJECT

Happy clown toy

The clown doll uses the blue and white stripes of the fabric cleverly to suggest the clown's body and limbs.

Materials, tools and equipment
Blue and white striped cotton fabric
Small piece white fabric, small piece black felt
Needle, thread, pins, embroidery threads
Filling, knitting yarn for hair
Velvet ribbon for a bow

Method
Trace the diamond shape and cut 16 papers **(1)**. The clown doll has 8 diamonds for his back and 8 for his front **(2)**. Cut 3 fabric diamonds 9mm (⅜in) larger all round with the stripes running vertically. Mount the patches and sew them together **(3)**. Cut 2 more diamonds for arms with the stripes running horizontally. Join these to the body shape **(4)**. Cut 3 diamonds from white fabric for the face and collar. Join these to the body **(5)**. Make up the clown's back in the same way. Join the back and front round the edges, the right sides of the patchwork facing, but leaving the 2 sides of the head diamond unstitched **(6)**. Take out the backing papers. Turn the clown right side out through the head. Stuff the body and head and sew up the head seams **(7)**. Embroider the features in Stem stitch **(8)**. Cut 30 strands of wool, 150mm (6in) long and tie in the middle. Sew to the top of the head. Cut some of the strands short for a fringe **(9)**. Make a velvet bow and sew across collar **(10)**. Cut two triangles from black felt and sew to feet **(11)**.

Other toys to make

The clown is only one of the amusing doll shapes you can make from diamond patchwork. Cut some diamond shapes from coloured paper and lay them on a sheet of white paper, moving them about in new arrangements. Cut some of the paper diamonds in half to make triangles. You will soon discover different ways of joining the shapes. For instance, the same arrangement of diamonds as that used for the clown would make a fish, if you used a green and blue fabric with a pattern to suggest the scales. You could perhaps embroider the fins and tail on a plain-coloured fabric. Add 2 diamonds to each side of the clown shape and you have a flying bird. Soft toys like this will make gifts for both adults and children – and, if you use a washable fabric and stuffing, they can also be given to babies.

PROJECT

Purse of diamonds

The fabric from which the diamond patches were cut was patterned with big, splashy flowers in reds, pinks and purples. By carefully placing the transparent template, a gradual blending of colours is achieved in the finished patchwork.

Materials, tools and equipment

30cm (12in) patterned fabric and the same in lining fabric
Diamond template set [25mm (1in)]
Purse clasp
Tracing paper, pencil,
Scissors, basting thread, matching threads, needle, pins

Method

Cut 25 backing papers from the solid template **(1)**. Cut 25 fabric diamonds from the transparent template [or 9mm (⅜in) larger all round than the paper templates]. Mount and join the patches to the shape of the purse. There will be some wastage of patchwork on the sides, but patches must be sewn in even if you need only a corner **(2)**. Make up enough patchwork for the front and back of the purse, or for the front only with a plain fabric for the back. Draw the purse pattern up from the graph pattern. The scale is 1 square to 10mm (7/16in). Lay the pattern on the patchwork, pin and cut out the shape with 9mm (⅜in) extra all round **(3)**. Cut out the backing and then cut out two linings in the same way **(4)**. You will see from the shape that there is a kind of collar at the top of the purse. This is the part which you will eventually sew to the clasp. Pin the purse front and back together, the right sides facing. Baste

from just under the collar on the left hand side to the same point on the right, leaving the top of the purse open. Baste about 9mm (⅜in) from the edge. Now sew on the same seam line, using either a sewing machine or by hand using backstitch. Take out the basting **(4)**. Sew the two pieces of lining together in the same way, pinning and basting them first, right sides of fabric facing. Trim the seam allowances of the purse to about half, and snip into it round the curved bottom edge. This is so that the purse turns to the right side neatly without a bulky seam. Turn right side out and press. Trim the seam allowance of the lining to about half and push into the purse, using a pencil to position it neatly **(5)**. Turn the top edges of the purse to the inside and pin and then baste. Take the clasp and open it. Position it on the outside of the purse. Start to sew the purse to the clasp by hand. The needle should be brought through from the back through a hole in the clasp, go into the purse immediately under the hole and then be brought back through the next hole alongside. Start with a knot and finish tightly with a double stitch on the wrong side **(6)**. Sew both sides of the clasp to the purse, taking care not to catch in the lining. Finally, turn the collar part of the lining under and neatly hem to the inside of the purse, just below the edge of the clasp.

Star of Bethlehem

This quilt design is famous, probably the best known of the patchwork patterns based on diamonds. It is called The Star of Bethlehem **(1)** and is traditionally worked in blue and white. Here the designer has used assorted red and brown patterned fabrics – probably the gleanings of her pieces bag – but the effect is charming and not over-colourful. Sometimes, Star of Bethlehem patterns are based on a central 6-point star but this quilt uses an 8-point star which makes the starburst larger. Large and small squares of white calico are fitted between the star clusters **(2)** and the quilting of the finished coverlet is worked in diamonds following the lines of the seams **(3)**. The Star of Bethlehem is sometimes worked as an almost circular piece of patchwork, diamonds being round a central star. Colours are bright, sometimes toning from a brilliant red central star to a pale yellow at the edge, or with a pale centre gradually deepening and brightening to orange, flame red and russet tones towards the edges. These pieces of patchwork look brilliant in worked silk fabrics and make beautiful stool covers or covers for round cushions. They have also been used to make wall coverings and circular rugs, worked in fine wool fabrics.

Borders

The border to this antique quilt is a band of the red fabric with 4 squares set at the corners, 2 red and 2 white. An alternative border, which uses the diamonds, might be plain white with 2 rows of diamonds set along the centre.

Applying borders

Cut strips of the border fabric 50mm–100mm (2–4in) wide depending on the effect you want. Joint the strips with straight seams. Lay the quilt on the floor or table, backing uppermost. Pin and baste the border fabric along one long edge, right side down and matching edges. Cut the excess fabric off and stitch about 12mm (½in) from the edge. Fold the strip out flat and lay the next strip in position. Baste and machine as before. Work all four sides in the same way. Turn the quilt over. Fold the strip border over onto the top side of the quilt. Turn under a narrow hem and hemstitch. Mitre the corners as you come to them and hem them neatly.

Hints on making the quilt

Work only one star block at a time. Cut only as many diamonds as you need for one block. The central star has 8 red diamonds, 16 white diamonds are set around it, and 24 red diamonds make the outer burst. Make up all the star blocks and then arrange them in position on a table top, or on the floor, so that you can plan the size of the linking squares. The small squares are framed with 4 red and 4 white diamonds, the larger squares being framed by the same patches.

Baubles

These beautiful hanging baubles are made with the usual patchwork technique, but the backing papers are left in position after the patches are sewn together.

Tools, materials and equipment
For the pentagon bauble
Pentagon template 37mm (1½in)
Thin, silky surfaced fabrics, yellow, lilac, cream, pale orange
Scraps of felt, bright pink, tan, orange
Silver and bronze petal-shaped sequins
Medium-sized pearl beads
Tiny beads in silver, gold and black
Strong thread for a hanger
Needle and sewing threads, thin stiff cardboard, dressmaker pins.

Method
Cut 12 templates from the thin card. Cut the fabric patches 9mm (⅜in) larger all round. Mount the patches on the backing cards with basting stitches but without taking the needle through to the right side of the patch. Sew the pentagon shapes into a ball from the right side **(1)**. To decorate, pick up

beads on the pins and push them into the seams **(2)**. Cut petals from the pink felt to make flowers. Push pins through the pearl beads and pin the petals to the ball. Cut circles of tan felt with pinking shears and pin to the ball with an orange flower and sequins **(3)**. Work out some decorative effects of your own and pin a different motif on each of the pentagon facets.

For the star bauble

25mm (1in) wide lozenge diamond template

Thin, silky fabrics, patterned and plain colours

Bronze and brass beads, medium-sized and small

Bronze-coloured flower-shaped beads

Long pins, needle, thread, thin cardboard, scissors, gold braid for hanging

Method

Cut 60 diamond shapes from the thin card. Cut fabric diamonds 9mm (3/8in) larger all round. 5 patches make one section of the star **(4)** and there are 12 sections. Each section is made up separately. Sew 5 diamonds into a star **(5)**. Sew the star into a cup shape by joining the last seam **(6)**. Assemble the star in two halves. Join 5 stars round a central star **(7)** and then join the two halves together. Push beads into seams and into the centre on pins.

Making the hanger The pentagon ball has a beaded hanger and a tassel of gold beads underneath.

The hanger can be stitched to the top of the ball in the same way as for the star, or it can be fastened to the top pentagon when the ball is being constructed. To do this, tie a knot in strong thread and push on a large bead. Bring the needle through the pentagon from the wrong side, so that the bead and knot secure the thread. Thread on circles of coloured felt and push them down to lie on top of the pentagon. Thread beads and make a loop at the end of the thread.

Log Cabin pattern

Log Cabin is a traditional American pieced patchwork pattern, made by applying strips of fabric round a centrally-set square.

Materials, tools and equipment

Cotton fabric in light and dark colours, about half patterned and half plain
Plain fabric for a foundation square
Calico for backing
Sewing thread, needle (or sewing machine)
Scissors, card for templates, pencil

Method

Draw a block plan first. Draw a 250mm (10in) square on paper. Divide it into four diagonally. Measure and draw a

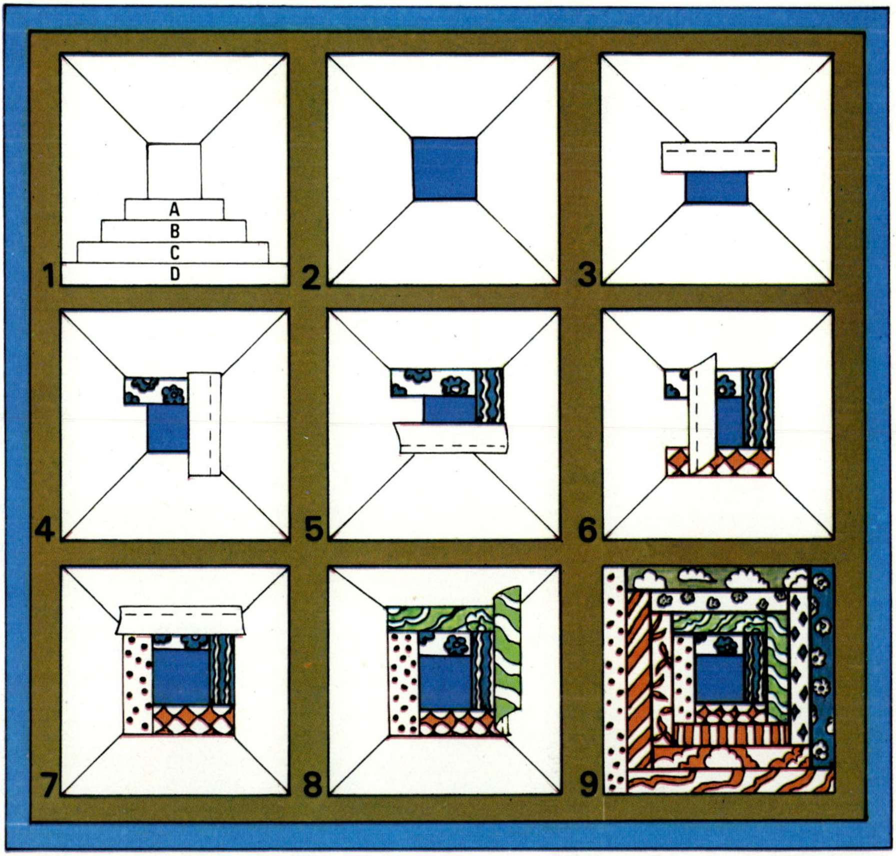

50mm (2in) square in the middle. Now divide the bottom triangle of the square into four horizontally. The lines should be 30mm (1¼in) apart. You now have the pattern for cutting the card templates for the foundation squares, the backing squares, and for the four strips which make up the Log Cabin pattern A, B, C, D **(1)**.

To make one block Mark a backing square diagonally with pencil lines or with basting stitches. Cut a foundation square and baste it to the middle of the backing **(2)**. Cut the first four strips with template A (the shortest), 2 from light fabric, 2 from dark. Lay the first light strip right side down on the foundation square, raw edges matching. Baste in position. Machine stitch or hand sew using running stitches 5mm (¼in) from the edge **(3)**. Press the strip back to the right side with the fingers. Lay light strip 2 along the next side of the foundation square, overlapping strip 1 **(4)**. Baste and stitch and press the strip back to the right side. Now the dark toned strips are used. Strip 3 and strip 4 are applied and stitched in the same way **(5, 6)**. For the next round of strips, use the second largest template, B, (2nd down in the plan) **(7)**. The third round of strips is cut with template C **(8)**. Continue using light on light strips and dark on dark, adding strips until you have worked 4 rounds **(9)**. A 5mm (¼in) seam allowance for joining blocks is left on all four sides.

Piped cushion

A beautifully made cushion deserves to be made up properly, with a piped edge. Piping is a tube or casing of fabric with cotton cord inside it, set into the seams of a cushion to improve the appearance.

Materials, tools and equipment
1m (1yd) of 90cm (36in) fabric for piping casing to match cushion cover
Medium to thin piping cord to fit round the cushion pad plus 75mm (3in)
Square cushion pad
Needle, thread, sewing machine
Scissors, long ruler, chalk pencil

Method
Cut cushion backing to the same size as the prepared front **(1)**. Lay the square of piping fabric flat. Lay the ruler across the fabric from corner to corner. Chalk along the edge of the ruler. You have marked the fabric along the bias. Measure another line, 31mm (1¼in) away.
Mark and rule another line 31mm (1¼in) away and continue until you have marked the square of fabric into strips **(2)**. Cut the strips up. If you pull them between your fingers you will see that they stretch. This stretch will enable the finished casing to curve round the corners of the cushion cover. Join enough strips to fit round the cushion cover.
The strips are joined on the bias like this. Lay one strip at an angle on the table, right side up. Lay another strip at an angle right side down, across the first strip so that the two ends are lying aligned in a straight line. Pin the strips together about 12mm (½in) from their aligned ends. Then baste and stitch on the line where the pins were. When you

open up the strips they are joined with a diagonal seam and you have made the piping casing.

Lay the piping cord along the middle of the piping casing **(3)**. Fold and work tiny running stitches to hold the cord in position, working the stitches as close as possible to the hidden cord **(4)**.

Lay the backing fabric on the table. Lay the piping cord in its casing round the edge, matching the raw edges of the casing and the cushion. As you arrange the piping round the corners, snip into the casing at this point to help it to curve round. Pin the casing in position and then baste it. The ends should overlap as shown in the middle of a side **(5)**. Lay the cushion cover front on top, right side down. Pin, matching the corners. Baste along the same basting line as that holding the casing in position. Put the piping foot on the machine and stitch along the edge of the piping cord (you will be able to feel it through the layers of fabric). Leave a gap in the seam for turning the cushion **(6)**. Trim the seam allowances and cut the corners off diagonally so that, when the cushion is turned right side out, the corners are neat and the seams are not too bulky. Put in the cushion pad and close the open seam with oversewing. Remove all the basting stitches carefully.

Rhodes Roundabout

The Rhodes Roundabout technique is the invention of a clever needlewoman who teaches patchwork – Frances Rhodes. The Roundabout is based on the same principle as the Log Cabin, but the foundation patch is an octagon and the final shape is round rather than square.

Materials, tools and equipment
Octagon-shaped motif from a printed fabric or a patch cut with a 60mm (2½in) diameter hexagon template
Plain and patterned fabrics
Foundation fabric
Sewing machine (optional), needle, sewing threads, basting thread, pins, scissors, tape measure

Method
Cut the foundation fabric to the size and approximate shape of the finished cushion. Baste the octagon patch to the middle of the foundation **(1)**. Measure one side of the octagon and cut 8 strips from your first choice of fabric, 3 times the measurement × 25mm (1in) wide. Take a strip and lay it on the octagon patch. Right sides of fabric should be facing and the raw edge of the strip exactly aligned along the octagon edge **(2)**. Baste the strip in position and then stitch (by machine or by hand using small running stitches) about 4mm (³⁄₁₆in) from the edge. Turn the strip back to the right side and press it down with the fingers. Take the next strip and lay it over the stitched strip and again aligning with the next

side of the octagon. Baste and stitch as before and turn the strip over to the right side. Continue working round the octagon until all 8 sides have been worked.
For the next round, choose a different fabric. Measure the side of the new hexagon and cut 8 strips 3 times the length by 25mm (1in). Once you have become a little practised you will not need to sew right along the strip. Simply start stitching just before the point where two strips cross and stop just after the side of the hexagon. The ends of the strip are then trimmed off **(3)**.
The cushion illustrated has 7 rounds altogether, and from round 4 the strips are deeper. Try cutting strips 37mm, 50mm and then 62mm (1½in, 2in, and then 2½in) deep **(4)**.

The Rhodes Roundabout is perfect for making round cushions.

Making a round cushion
The back of the cushion is cut in two pieces. Measure the diameter of the cushion, draw a circle on paper and cut it in half. Use a half pattern and pin it to doubled fabric. Cut round the curve of the half circle, adding 12mm (½in) for seam allowance but add 75mm (3in) on the straight edge. Turn a 12mm (½in) hem, and then another 12mm (½in), on both straight edges. Arrange them overlapping so that together they make a full circle. Baste the two pieces together and make the cushion up with the front in the usual way. The cushion pad is inserted through the overlap. Sew on two press studs for closures.

Suffolk puffs

Suffolk puffs is the traditional name for this technique but it is known by other names in different parts of Britain and in America. There is almost no sewing to do and this is the kind of patchwork that would make a group project for sewers of different ages.

The fabrics used for a Suffolk puff quilt can be mixed – cotton, silk, velvet, and rayon, man-made fibre fabrics of all kinds but they should be of similar weight and soft enough to gather.

Materials, tools and equipment

Assorted fabrics
A saucer or small plate
Soft pencil or chalk pencil
Scissors, needle, strong thread
Backing fabric

Method

Lay fabric right side up and mark out circles using a saucer or plate as a guide. Keep the marked circles close together to be economical of fabric **(1)**.

Press a narrow hem to the wrong side with the fingers and run a gathering thread all round the edge **(2)**.

Pull the gathering thread as tightly as possible and knot the ends **(3)**. Flatten the puffs with the hand **(4)**.

To plan the colour scheme of a quilt, draw circles with a small cup or a round bottle cap. Colour the circles to match the fabrics you intend to use. Mark in linking lines where the circles touch **(5)**. To join puffs, hold two puffs together, thread needle with mercerized thread and work four or five oversewing stitches in one spot. Puffs are joined together in four places **(6)**.

Stitch the finished puff quilt to the backing fabric at the edges, using oversewing stitches. Work a few stitches at intervals over the quilt catching the two layers together.

Puff quilts

Another kind of puff quilt
Cut circles of fabric and seam two together, right sides facing, leaving a gap in the seam for turning to the right side.
Turn and stuff with Terylene filling, not too tightly. Close the seam. Make a number of puffs and sew them together with oversewing stitches. The quilt is lightweight and very warm.

Other things to make
The quilt illustrated is made of shiny and dull-surfaced fabrics, some patterned some plain. The gathered side has been used uppermost here but sometimes the plain side is used. If a fabric with a single flower motif were used and the flower set in the middle of a puff, the effect would make a beautiful shawl. You would need about 250 puffs to make a triangular shawl – approximately 3m (3yds) of assorted fabrics. Puffs could also be used to decorate a fabric belt or to make a gay bolero jacket **(7)**.

Cathedral window

Cathedral window is not really a patchwork technique but it does use patches of fabric and the result is often used to make beautiful quilts. The stained glass effect is made by arranging the folded edges of fabric over a patch of a contrasting colour or pattern. The foundation fabric is folded twice and the thickness of the finished 'patch' means that there is no need to back a quilt made of Cathedral windows.

Materials, tools and equipment
Soft, cotton fabric for the foundation
Patterned or coloured fabric for the windows
Scissors, tape measure, sewing threads, pins and needles

Method
Cut two 150mm (6in) squares of the foundation fabric. Turn a narrow hem on all four sides of each and press **(1)**. Measure and mark the centre of the square. Fold each of the corners to the centre and pin **(2)**. Now fold the corners of the new square to centre again **(3)**. Remove the first pins and pin anew. Work the second square in exactly the same way and sew the two squares together with oversewing **(4)**.

Make the 'window'. Cut a 42mm (1¾in) square of the contrasting fabric. Pin it over the seam joining the two folded

squares **(5)**. The next stage must be done carefully. Take out the pins. Lift the folded edge that you can just see under the edge of the coloured square of fabric. Turn it over onto the coloured square so that the folded edge becomes a curved fold.

The four folded edges brought over onto the patch become a curved frame – the 'window'. Hold the fold in place between finger and thumb of the other hand, and work tiny running stitches along the curved fold, taking stitches right through the folded fabric, the coloured patch and the foundation backing **(6)**. Fold and stitch each in the same way and then, finally, secure at the corners with one or two small stitches **(7)**.

Work windows in pairs in this way and then join pairs with oversewing, window sides facing each other.

Cathedral window patchwork should not be pressed.

Crazy patchwork

Crazy patchwork is a technique which can use quite small scraps of fabric. The pieces are stitched to a foundation material and the resulting patchwork is quite strong. In this type of patchcraft, fabrics of different types can be mixed and used together but if you are using very thin materials, such as voile or lawn, they should be mounted on muslin before using them with heavier fabrics.

Designing Crazy patchwork appears quite easy to put together but in fact, matching the colours and textures harmoniously takes a bit of designing. Before starting to sew it is a good idea to cut pieces to approximate shape and move them around on the foundation fabric to see the effects of contrast.

The basic method

Whether you are making a block of crazy patchwork for a quilt, or making a whole quilt, the basic technique is the same. Cut the foundation fabric to size. (Choose new sheeting for a foundation – it is a better investment in the long run.) Cut the first patch to fit a right-angled corner. Pin to the foundation and then work running stitches round the straight edges about 3mm (⅛in) from the edge, leaving the crazy edge 'free'. Cut the next patch and tuck one edge under the first patch. Pin it down and then work running stitches to hold the second patch under the first patch, again leaving the crazy edge free **(1)**. Keep adding patches and stitching **(2)**

until you have covered the foundation fabric. To finish, all the raw edges are covered up with embroidery. Chain stitch **(3)** and Feather stitch **(4)** are traditional crazy patchwork stitches. Alternatively, machine zigzag stitches can be worked over the edges **(5)**.

Machine-stitched crazy patchwork
If you have a swing-needle machine, crazy patchwork can be put together very quickly. Arrange the scraps on the foundation fabric and baste them in position – or simply use pins. Set the machine to a wide, fairly open zigzag and work over all the raw edges.

Crazy patchwork poncho
Make up two rectangles of patchwork 750 × 370mm (30 × 15in). Lay the two rectangles on the table and mark the corners of one rectangle, 1, 2 on the top edge, 3, 4 on the bottom edge. Mark the second rectangle 5, 6 on the top edge, 7, 8 on the bottom edge. These numbers are for joining the rectangles into the poncho shape. Pin the poncho together by matching numbers like this: match corners 3 and 6, with the edges of both pieces together. Pin and baste, right sides facing. Now join corners 2 and 4 to 5 and 6, edges matching. Pin and baste. Stitch both seams. Cut 2 lining pieces to the same size as the poncho pieces and join them in the same way. Put the finished lining over the patchwork, right side of the lining to the right side of the patchwork. Baste and stitch all round the hem and turn the poncho right side out. Finish the neckline with braid. Add wool fringing round the hem if you like.

PROJECT

Patchwork to wear

Once you can do patchwork, you can make some of the beautiful, colourful clothes that are often seen in expensive boutiques. Shirts, skirts, blouses, dresses, hats, bags – all these can be made of patchwork and the basic technique is really very easy.

When you are choosing a paper pattern for your patchwork garment, choose a design that is very simple in shape and does not have too many pieces. Patchwork is so bright and eyecatching in itself and anyway it is easier to work a few big pieces of patchwork than a number of small bits.

The first step is to find out how much patchwork you need for each piece of the pattern. Both sides of a jacket, such as the one illustrated, should have the same number of patches and the sides should match up. Take a piece of the paper pattern and using a soft pencil and a ruler, mark the piece into 25mm (1in) squares. Now copy the shape of the pattern piece on squared paper, reducing the scale. You might decide for instance that on 10mm (½in) squared paper, the scale was going to be 3 of your 25mm (1in) squares to one 10mm (½in) square. Still working to scale, draw the patches on your graph plan and colour them in **(1)**. You can instantly see how many patches of each colour you need, and the order in which you will sew them together. Cut your fabric patches and arrange on your paper pattern pieces to check position and fit **(2)**. Baste pieces together and sew together into strips **(3)**. When you have sewn the strips into

areas of patchwork, press and then use the patchwork as fabric in the normal way, pinning the paper pattern to it and cutting out for dressmaking **(4)**.

Machine patchwork
A swing needle sewing machine is very useful for patchwork when large areas are being made up. There are a few basic rules to remember, but otherwise the technique is simple – and very speedy!

Method of working
Mount the patches in the usual way. Prepare the sewing machine with size 14 (Continental No. 90) needle and use a mercerized thread, No. 50 or 60. Set the machine to a zigzag of 1½–2 and to medium stitch length. You may need to loosen the top tension a little. Experiment with the stitch on scraps of fabric before starting. Lay two patches together, right sides facing. Set the machine wheel so that the needle is going to swing to the left first. Position the needle piercing the top right of the patches. As you slowly stitch, the stitches should pierce both patches on the left and go just outside them on the right. The last stitch should be to the right. Remove the work and tie off the ends of thread securely. The papers may be caught in the stitches but they should pull out quite easily.

Suede and leather Stitch suede and leather by simply butting unmounted patches together and zigzag the edges together working on the right side. It looks very effective.

Credits:
Page 8 Alexander Winsor. Page 38, Lorna Tull. Pages 12, 20, Tina Ealovega. Page 14, Sister E. Frazer. Pages 18, 22, 24, 46, 40, 60, 62, American Folk Art, London. Pages 26, 34, 44, Amanda Harlow. Page 30, Kemp Antiques, Horne, Surrey. Page 32, Jean Mott. Page 36, Anne Kingham and Lynette Merlin Syme. Page 48, Audrey Vincente Dean. Pages 50, 52, 54, Frances Rhodes. Page 58, Lynette Merlin Syme.

Useful addresses

Squared paper	Bourne & Hollingsworth Oxford Street London W1
Sewing accessories	John Lewis Oxford Street London W1
Patchwork templates	Needlewoman Shop 146 Regent Street London W1 (postal shoppers also)
Left-handed scissors	Anything Left Handed Shop 65 Beak Street London W1 (postal shoppers also)
Terylene fillings and wadding	John Lewis Oxford Street London W1
Fabrics for patchwork	Laura Ashley 71 Lower Sloane Street London SW1